AF323529

By Light Betrayed

PRAISE FOR SHERRY RENTSCHLER'S BOOKS

PAPER BONES

Five Star Review! "… a poet in the truest sense of the word…Her poems have the ability to both enchant and haunt the reader."
>--Tania Stanley for Readers' Favorite

"…tantalizes…challenges us….has the ability to give new meaning to a single word…is gifted at turning a phrase with double entendre that will take you by surprise."
>--Mary Deal, award-winning author of *River Bones* and *Write It Right.*

"These poems express the full panoply of poetic possibilities …an excellent poet…"
>--Rich Weatherly, poet and author of *Closed Doors, A Trilogy*

"Her work demonstrates a wide versatility, and her strong imagery evokes an expansive range of emotions."
>--Ginger Myrick, author of *Insatiable: A Macabre History of France*

"…thought-provoking…each (poem) will take you on a journey and leave you thinking, long after reading."
>--Regina Puckett, award-winning poet and author of *Regina Puckett's Complete Book of Poetry*

I WISH YOU JOY
(as Sheryl Rentschler)

"The spectacular photos in this book would be enough reason to recommend it…The author's talent to weave the story of her mother's love for her and their relationship makes this book much more than a photo book…"
>--Margie Miklas, journalist, photographer, travel blogger, author of *Memoirs of a Solo Traveler – My Love Affair with Italy.*

By Light Betrayed

Poetry of the Vampires

Sherry Rentschler

www.bookstandpublishing.com

Published by
Bookstand Publishing
Morgan Hill, CA 95037
4185_1

ISBN 978-1-61863-939-4 (paperback)
ISBN 978-1-61863-940-0 (hardcover)
ISBN 978-1-61863-990-5 (epub)

Library of Congress Control Number: 2014914850

Because of the dynamic nature of the Internet, any web addresses or links contained in this book may have changed since publication and may no longer be valid. The views expressed in this work are solely those of the author and do not necessarily reflect the views of the publisher, and the publisher hereby disclaims any responsibility for them.

Cover design © Travis Miles 2014
Interior photography © Sherry Rentschler 1975, 1976, 2009-2014
(except where noted as Shutterstock)
Author photograph © Amanda Goforth Photography

Printed in the United States of America

FOR ANYONE
WHO HAS PAUSED
IN THE DARK AND SAID,
"UM…DID YOU HEAR *THAT*?"

Contents

Preface

Vampires come to us from every continent around the globe. They are called by as many names as there are different countries, names such as upir, strigoi, vampyr, hannya, and mullo. Initially, the vampire frightened us. His visage (most often male) was hideous and terrifying. Born from the grave, he roamed the world seeking an existence through sustenance in blood. Each of these creatures carried the stench and the rot of Death. We cowered before them.

As time went on, we personalized the vampire, made him seductive and beautiful instead of horrifying and hideous. We gave him exotic names and lovely flesh as we turned red, piercing eyes into fathomless wells of mystery and temptation. We romanticized and desired the undead.

Today's glamorized legends and myths fill our social consciousness, our entertainment, and our fantasies. We are so enamored that we buy items such as perfume, lipstick, movies, clothing, and bed linens in support of the vampire tales we read. Truthfully, most of us are fans of the vampire, whether or not we admit it, whether we believe in the reality or not.

As a fan, I must ask, what if you are right? What if the vampire is real and beautiful? What if his muse aches to express the poetry of his exotic life, or lack of it? Would the inner secrets of the vampire-poet be less meaningful if he told you the truth? Would you ache less if he held you at twilight and told you of his suffering before he "made his point?" Because we crave them, my answer to the last is, I think not!

Therefore, I offer to you the poetry of the vampires, one voice in particular, many in thought. Their words will seduce your dreams. They will make promises born of your desires and sated on their whims. Generally a somber lot, they can be a bit cheeky, too. But I warn you, they do not mourn who they are or wish they were human again. Their tears are for you because they would make you one of them. Would *you*? Assuming the fiction becomes truth, I present what I believe represents their souls in verse.

Yours between the lines,
Sherry Rentschler
July 2014

Acknowledgements

I am fortunate to find wonderful people who mentor, create, and advise along the way. I can't name everyone who kept me sane or who answered my endless questions, however, I do wish to thank some special people.

Travis Miles, cover designer, created a magical vision. I am so grateful.

Sean Foley, friend and graphic artist, who performed emergency surgery of the artistic sort and never complained, no matter the hour.

My three Muse-ateers! Mary and Andrea Newton, along with Brianna Paglia for being ready with emergency assistance, a bit of research or some laughter.

Christy Nelson, beta reader, who kept me from dashing my computer against the wall.

Melonie Flomer, kindred spirit, who created the poem title years ago when the vampires first emerged. I thought it would make a great book title!

I thank the influencers, the "author gods" of my favorite vampire legends: Bram Stoker, Sheridan Le Fanu, Richard Matheson, Kim Newman, Anne Rice, Suzy McKee Charnas, and new favorites Christopher Farnsworth, Kim Harrison, and Jim Butcher.

Finally, never least or last, to my husband Ron, who understands my desire for endless twilight, and for supplying the coffee, tea, chocolate, space, time and patience. Thank you for being my vampire. Forever will never be enough.

Introduction

I am your Vampire.

I am your dreams, your nightmares, and your darkest secrets. My words are my fingers. Let me describe the path my fingers will take when I memorize the divinity of your flesh and sing you our songs.

From your temple, I will outline a delicate line across to your eyes, those eyes eagerly searching mine for the question you are anxious to ask, the_one I am forbidden to breathe. With your first blink, I will drift down to the rise of your cheekbone - an erotic symbol of a body's supple hip – tracing my nail inward to the tender curl of your puckered lip. I will linger like a moth hovering near the breathy, waiting space, then pass over your disappointed sigh, down to the tiny cleft in your chin.

A lone finger will follow your nervous swallow into the curve of your neck, past the nestled Eve's apple to the sweet hollow of fragile, twin collarbones. Anxiously my body will bend you to me, absorbing your quivering limbs as a bowstring pulled taught, then strung.

If you are the weapon then I am your hunter, eager to pull you, my bow. If you are the harp, then I will strum you until you find passion's etude. All the while, my lips will repeat the memory of the finger's adventure. Your gaps make me hesitate before I lift you closer, tighter, higher as I, impatient lover, ride the pulsing vein into the hollow of your neck's shadow.

Our adieu is artfully predictable; your palatable surprise, a boredom. The lullaby I leave you in this satiation is the loudest silence you will ever know. I promise to set you free in an imagined, long-dreamt release somewhere between fantasy and nightmare. The passion is all yours for the claiming if you do not struggle.

Will you be the one to resist the last temptation of a sanguine forever? Who can remain with so little and surrender entirely, knowing the moment of my passion is the coldest night of all? Is it you? Then I beg you to release me now, lay bare your body in trust. When the kisses slow and my mouth lingers, I dare you not to quiver, not to whisper my name, or moan with a longing to cry out. I beg you to swallow the scream you'll ache to give as the first lethargy claims your heart, and passes from your body into mine.

What competitions could there be, that you would dare your breath against the weight of my hunger? The smile you give to me from this single naiveté, I will endure before the last flutter of your beautiful, curled lashes. I will stuff your fingers full of crushed rose petals to perfume the rotted gloom.

Finally, I will take you beyond Love's lie. We have no need, you and I, of false promises murmuring of forever. The words I offer will whisper of the love I can never know, the lust only I may give in requiem, and the tango we will create from a single night.

We have only this moment to leech our souls together.

These words are my promise, like my kiss.

Come with me into the the dreaming nocturne. Surrender.

No matter how hard you fight the darkness, every light casts a shadow, and the closer you get to the light, the darker that shadow becomes.

— Plato, *Critias*

By Light Betrayed

Cusp Moment

6:47 p.m.
Sun-tickled treetops
tantalize and fade -
the elegant sneer.

Shadows birthing or escaping
under a golden flicker of flesh tones,
hues of forgotten daytime blood
herald cold diffusion on puckered lips,

dusky relief and deliverance.
Drink the sky, swallow, and pass on.
Twilight's teasing; don't be late.

Ghost Life

It's never enough, though I try.
Happiness is our illusion; so is love.
Words bleed and your flesh is cold.
When will I cease to be a ghost?
I want to feel beyond this pain
where sacrifices are made for me,
not for some illusion.
Deceptive eyes appear to crave
then blink instead, and covertly
turn away, thinking I don't know
or won't care to see beyond deceit.
I see more than you imagine.
I even feel the separation,
though I have lied about this, too.
"Come to me," the voices whisper,
and I do, to slink away in
exquisite torment, my blood a river
where I can drown in solitude.
Let's pretend that you do love me
and make a happy shroud of longing -
you for that one, me for you.
I'll keep my private aching silent (like a grave).
I'll tell you what you need to hear (eulogize),
and murmur kindly, give you peace.
Never mind the blaspheme you write
on my eager heart, lips trembling
over words you swear in love.
I am a ghost of what you really want.

When I am gone, you'll turn from turbulence
to quiet happiness, the most precious of my dreams.
Exorcised of me, I become your best memory,
and the worst for me is you'll remain
a vessel for the passion I once knew.
Ghosts can't really feel now, can they?
Close the scrapbook; come to me.
You'll cry, "I love you, my only apparition."
Then, "yes, I know," I will lie.

The Execution

Cremate me and stop weeping
for embalmed love.
Take this heart; set it by the door,
a blighted souvenir
untouched by death.
Cut out my eyes, made into windows,
prisms for refracted light,
damnation darkened
from soulless delusion.
Place these hands on my shameful chest
where music swelled, concealing
a cavern of faded harmonies
sustained in echoes.
Remove your ring from a stiffened hand
where kisses rested and passion faltered.
Face me north so moon and sun
do heroic battle over my left
and nearly right.
Place me brutally unseeing but aware.
Close the coffin.
Leave faithless lips alone - cold enough
without cryptic breath and debased misery.
Don't kiss them.
They feel chapped from faith discarded
in sublime lust and taste of ash.

By Light Betrayed

Smoke curls across horizon's canvas,
obscuring us from the firestorm of our memories.
Don't look back, my love.

We're miles away from our grave of sighs;
and too close to that bridge of regret.
Look now and you will singe from the pyres
or weep from falling cinders of nascent hope.
The abyss is too dark to be revealing.
Either you will tumble into despairing canyons
or unwitting, find the buried apathy within.
Yes, we set the blaze, unknowing
love is a furious spark and flash.
Oh, this passage was an impasse we ignored,
too blind to smell the kerosene of sabotage
or easily handle betrayal's tinder.
We have shades of truth to light the way ahead;
besides, the smoke is black as befits a shroud.

We will outlive the inevitable dawning 'morrow
to build a new crossing beyond eternity's bend.
Sunset cowers at shadows deepening;
our history is razed in the denouement.
Don't look back, my love!

Stone Cold

They stared
at the guardians, the angels,
the stone turrets, the miniature houses
with eagles and doves, dragons
and demons. Scratching and scraping,
the metal doors screeched as steel
scarred concrete in a final protest.

They stared
in embarrassed, morbid silence;
inept, sorrowful, shallow, inadequate
for the occasion. Patting and weeping,
they christened with tears, wailing,
flailing, sobbing and fainting;
black crows poised over carrion at a kill.

They stared
as the sepulcher groaned, a horrid
resigned sigh, the welder's torch
hissing, flaming, melting cool metal,
scaring death into silence. Air forced
into stagnation, suddenly pungent,
swallowed but one scream as
they stared.

Oh whOle nOte

YOur
thrOat
hOlds
On
tO
mOre
lOud,
rOund,
sO
sOft
sOund.
LegatO.
LentO.
O
wOman
Of
blOOd,
O
pastOrale
Of
hOpe!
GO
slOw,
nOw
fOrte,
lOst
sOng
Of
passiOn.
PrOfOund.
SwallOwed.
DOne.
TwO
bOld
whOle
nOtes,
nOw
One
O.

The Vow

When I hold her, she is soft and pliant,
yielding but not abdicating,
passion cut on desire,
dangerous obsession.
When she holds me, I am cold and immobile,
yielding but so demanding,
passion cut on desire,
dangerous possession.
Her seduction is the lack of guile,
sweetly wanton and wanting.
My seduction is the flow of blood,
bitterly practiced and promising.
Will she scream when the last gasp
renders all her dreams into
terrible and terminal reality, or
will I laugh when the first gasp
delivers her reality into delicious
and delirious dreams?
I may kill her, unfortunately, eventually,
and she will take my death and
give her life that I might die again
in company, alone.
She will birth me, ultimately, finally,
and I will give her life and
take my death that she might live again
in crowded solitude.
You must ask for it; I need to believe.
I must answer for it; you need to know.
Together we'll dance unseen in
shadow and blood, misunderstood
and forgiven, hungry.
This is eternity where you were always mine
but I was never yours. Somewhere in between,
the possibilities became meaningless,
an almost elegant wonderment of
"until death do we part,"
for a taste of her lips, in a hope
of her yesterday,
for a drink of my tears, in a despair
of my tomorrow.

Neighborhood of Bones

Granite gray and bark brown hues
color stairs and halls of nature's gothic rooms.
Weathered, skeleton driveways edge dead flowers
dropped by strangers suffocating on blame,
drowning in quiet, guilt suffused.
Silence, the immortal doorbell, announces
newcomers passing from the past, unearthing
a Nob Hill of sepulcher mansions
where moneyed death buys sanctuaries
of prominence and permanence.
Eerily mediocre beside the unmarked,
all shades illuminate similarly, identity lost
to lives, ravaged, stolen with eternal disregard.
Dead, undead, remarkable in the unremarked
tombstones. As foretold, no one cares
in the neighborhood of bones.

A Point to Never

Shadows make edges in the mayhem,
improving our perception of life.
Hear the trolleys electric tango on the wires.
Feel the wax paper cups and cheap paper napkins
forgotten in the shaded stairwell.

Touch the chain swaying hastily
on a scarred and open doorway.
Bloodied roses, the acrid perfume,
lingers, wafting from silky sheets
smelling of a concubine's betrayal.

Eyes seek beyond the gilded patina,
eager for a last, fulfilling surrender.
Don't search around shadows,
or inside expectant hearts.
Illusion is a cheater's sixth sense
and a predator's second nature.

Catching Hell

When you're far away from me,
sometimes I do myself harm.
I junket among my memories
pretending I lie in your arms.
I kick at pieces of a broken heart,
(resurrecting the lost promises
time and distance rent apart),
while I tally up the losses.
I am midnight's sad mourner,
as amber-brown eyes turn to rust.
I am love's whimsical scorner,
as I shuffle through the mental dust.
Decay and neglect possess me,
(no love light shines in the dark),
stumbling by who I used to be
while straining to tear up my heart.
Can I survive on fortitude?
(or would that be cause for laughter?)
Must I partner with solitude?
(or does that come later, after?)
Poor, long-forgotten memories
and the silent tales they tell.
Your remnants I guard, so jealously,
when junketing in my private hell.

Venous Void

Underneath the fall,
grace quivers with expectation
and begs for self-righteous
forgiveness.
Cold hours for visions,
truth hovers without impunity
and commands transient
acceptance.
This is for the wasted,
the worn, and the deceived.
This is for the torn,
the fostered, and the conceived.
Now is for yesterday and
a tomorrow rife with "then,"
paid in flaxen-kissed wishes
for complacent beliefs --
cacophonous, vociferous,
mutely solicitous.
Spend all your heart coin;
toss away change.
The gutter is richer than mankind.
Lay down this truth for a lesser evil
bought for one lie, bittersweet.

'Twas the Blood Before New Year…

…and all through the meanest streets,
sugary blood echoed with dreams
buried in humanity's heartbeats.
She'd not traveled far, but took a stalking detour.
Her hunger had risen and there was only one cure.
While all the good children were nestled in bed,
she walked the wild streets, this undead redhead.
In the alleys she waited, green eyes glistening bright,
taking pleasure from the vilest in the dirty, foul night.
Over the rooftops she hunted, a cat to the mouse,
chasing her prey o'er each roof of each house.
She appeared as an angel, so porcelain, so pale,
and she purred like a kitten, so homeless and frail,
but just when you thought it was safe by her side,
her teeth found a home in your neck and your pride.
A dozen gifts she left at the orphanage door,
but the scurrilous janitor she left drained on the floor.
While back at the pub, the barmaid was tipped
for giving our "angel" a pro bono nip.
She disappeared on the wind (no "down" on this thistle),
and she preened at every gasp and throaty wolf whistle.
When all gifts were received, she rose up on the wind;
the vampire paused before heading home once again.
She called to the untouched and the unwary living,
"Thanks for your donations in this season of giving!"

Beloved

This word is all I have in silence.
Let my breath define it.
Let it forge the pyre of your heart,
trembling on your lips,
wishing it had died,
doubting it ever will.

I know your pain for it becomes me.
Every time you gasp I am reborn.
I know, too, you have forgotten
my presence here,
perpetual and petrified,
memory dismissed.

Look up.
Share the only landscape we are given,
celestial bed and dreamers folly.
Look down.
A feast in every vein, neglected, dry,
waiting to be fed with just a smile.

Look in.
Hear the syncopated beating,
the sigh that waits to finish,
incomplete across my lips.
Remembrance is a gift
and the ache that pains me.

If a shadow makes you blink,
or you wake from sleep and sigh,
if just once you hold your breath,
stand still and close your eyes.
I'm there.

Dining on the Twilight

Children! Awake from the day's elbow.
Cast away feather down for gossamer.
Monday's bells are silently screaming
as we fly down the subway tunnel,
prepared to dead end on Tomorrow's corner.
When the Ancients finally call for us,
humming their sleepy melodies,
remember, the first cut is only for the numbing.
True pain begins after the pause.
Too thin, this bridal veil disguised in sequins.
The party finished us eons past.
For this, they say, we sacrificed our virtue,
leaving dignity to rot before our tombstones.
Even thieves will barter lucre for a passion
traded in the brothels of the mourners.
Are we less for needing more than we can taste
when the candle is finally gutted
and our scalpels are laid to rest?
Mortals sleep against the bosom of their scrapbooks,
fearing nothing but their death after our breath.
They'll resurrect us in the yesterdays to follow,
craving us when their boredom is untenable.
Then from our marble tables we will answer -
a bridal vow, a venal bargain, sanctified,
while dining on the twilight and the marrow.
Outside, the demented memories blossom
as weeds to buckle under concrete minds.
No humanity will subjugate our consciousness.
They are addicts with no where left to hide.
Hurry! The dogs are baying and they hunger!
Put on your velvet gloves, deny the chalice!
When tomorrow fades, we go into their chambers -
embalmed with legend, weaned on fear, adored in
tattered books, stained to spite the dawn -
for the feast of ash and buried haste,
emerging sated and reborn.

My Pain of Joy

I stretch out my naked form, offering a feast of
scars and self-deluded fairy tales in puckered flesh.
The lessons have a purpose.
Trace with me the first hopeful mistake
around the toe that stumbled, too confident.
Follow, lost in vein, to the weakened ankle, a crescent
slice near tender tendons, and an artery leading
from Achilles to Gideon. Well-advanced, a calf,
defined from running, leads up the thigh
of thoughtless yearning, to the hip of rising hope;
and here a stuttering, stapled road where the
knife was not sharp enough. On the arm of
Last Embrace, a jagged line, playing close
to barbed wire hearts. A nicked finger wrote
blood on jagged windows, sterilized,
opening for happily-ever-after mornings.
Shadowed bruise of my wrist's reaching,
a little burn from passion's lustful fire.
Bare shoulders have not borne enough;
lashes cross the back in self-flagellating insight.
Here, the eye's corner, near blindness from love
eclipsing all others. You know the punishment
Icarus suffered; my fall was much less noble.
Down the curve of throated whispers, twin thumbprints,
a last offering in uncomfortable sacrifice,
a shared hope in a mouth's needful abandon,
one lick enough to cauterize wounded pride.
Advance fearlessly to the last and best.
The pale, (etched), scalpel runs rib to breastbone;
telltale damage never healed, though was toughened.
Caressed, new flesh quivers in rapt mistrust.
Untouched flesh is reserved for *you*.
A scar to tell a tale; a tale to carve a life.
In between the abject moments, bleeding remembers.
I offer half a chest of dreams, beautifully unmarred;
and all my soul to etch "once upon a time" undoing
before I forget to love you.

Nocturne
(for Nicolas)

Staccato,
the throat string,
a chord, tenuto,
fingered vibrato,
crimson andante,
passionate legato,
breathless caesura,
languid allegro,
pouring larghetto.
Ah, gasping crescendo
without refrain!
Your symphony,
and mine.

Crossing the Line

Sunlight teases behind the tomb.
Dandelions wilt against concrete.
I dance on sidewalk shadows,
Death between the lines.

Use the bones for witches' chalk.
Draw protective circles close.
Night enlivens our potency,
Death outside the lines.

Sleep controls the marionette.
Escape is paid in screams.
Our blood blurs our every hope,
Death across the lines.

Dead Born
(or The Sequel Under the Bed)

From ashes to ashes so the story lies;
breath of bone dust and ragged cobwebs,
frayed spider silk and angel dust,
dead skin and stray hair,
bent eyelash, cloven fingernail,
body of cockroach legs, moldy pollen,
blistered skin and crusted dandruff,
puckers of dried sweat, iron salt,
spittle spray and broken tooth.
Such shadows of bile, marrow and blood,
from ashes cast to ashes gasped,
to Omega from Alpha,
misbegotten echoes in coffin dirt.

Forgotten Flavors

I wept tears, hollow and empty,
tasteless and crystalline, shattering
like glass when you licked them,
little slivers piercing your closed heart,
unfelt - love was dead then.

Bitter blood tingles hopeless flesh
with mad mistrusting hallucinations.
Sighs of discord and regret quivered
through warm breath spiced with lust,
untouched - love was dead then.

"Creator of the poison apple!"
so you whispered, then bid me, bite.
My starved and bloodied palate tasted
withered memories in desire's marrow,
unmoved - love was alive then.

All our yesterdays evaporate from lips
chapped and blistered with neglect
where only a hungered tongue flicks
alive the savory scabs of tender yearning,
unremarkable - love lives there.

Unquiet Shadow

She used to be there, part shadow and part life.
My nights discomforted, despite our pairing.
When I read somewhere she was lost, missing,
my shroud became abysmal in its mocking.

Delicious cold, this fear that burns the blood.
Fragile were the rusted bones of her mortality.
Nothing fallow in the rose with decayed edges.
Those memories we buried without brutality.

I can't - won't - forget the winter of her making,
the mauves and purples of a twilight-broken season,
with endless moonlight made of wedding fire,
or the devouring in the blood beyond my reason.

We were ultimately betrayed and then deceived
before others gaping in horrified denial.
We've nothing left, no penance do we offer.
Ours is not the pain they put on trial.

From stone to stone we danced the jesters gamble,
and fool I was, now she drifts alone at night,
a tombstone in her mind's eye of forgetfulness;
a pale shadow of the woman I claimed in life.

Heart's Dream

I had a dream, a wish really,
with a violin on my knee.
Her fingers bloodied up the strings
and left their taste for me.
Her eyes oozed tears of misery,
luscious in their pain,
and when I played and sprayed her face,
she screamed for me again.
It is a dream without an end,
finished before it began.
But I'll raise the violin, you see,
and beg you, "play me" once again.
Dulcet voice that whispers low
of your desire in the rough,
come take the violin's place
until we both are bled enough.

Royal Street

Time is for memories, frayed recollections,
fraught with our chaos and short on regret.
We are the remnants of innocent wishes
lost in the pavement, too sharp to forget.
You were the player and I, the recorder,
watchful and curious cast as the inevitable
disappointment and sorrow for the hypocrite -
outsider pulled inside, incontrovertible.
For all the missed chances - the stupors and failings -
let this be forgiveness if never forgotten,
the rancor absolved in the cloves and the pernod,
our absinthe – our pride – brought us to the fallen.
The rose-colored glasses were never myopic;
though our vision was muted, the blood remained red.
This is our memory, our poem, our finale:
a stain on a handkerchief, a last folly, undead.

Sanguineous Gift

Cold and granite stillness
presses tangible and tactile folds
of flesh beyond the tearing skin,
licking, lapping into orgasmic pleasure,
as twilight eyes wail with muted pain.

Stretched across marble altar's lap,
pulsing body, worshipped by velvet fingers,
is revered and puckered dreamily under
a devilish kiss of smothered eagerness
until unrepentant, dismal life is lost.

Below bisque and porous angel tears,
obscenity charades over passion's womb
for blood sacrificed in fettered haste,
as unlamented souls, in unrequited life,
surrender for a tomb, eternally embraced.

To the Bone

One, outlaw, trickle of blood
slips and crawls,
drooling between cold breast's flesh.
Ecstasy and pain misuse one another,
as the void embalms the spirit,
as darkness embraces despair
with sneering eagerness.
Nipples lactate with enflamed desire.
Fingers wither to grasp
what cannot be held –
echoing, gasping breath.
Black pupils, floating beneath watered crimson,
beg forgiveness, craving candied promises
born of salted fear.
Nape hairs bristle with decadence.
Blind dreams cannot smell
ageless Death's perfumed stench.
Lips abandon their sighs
as the last scarlet tear quivers,
lurching past the breast bone
covering the soul.

First Bite
(*or Adam's Apple*)

An eyelash falls within a tear.
I noticed its delicately colored edges,
not unlike your innocent mouth
painted pink like unripened, virgin fruit.

The salted crystal trickles
by the corners of this tender plum.
I steal a lick, a taste of nectar,
before daring to lap the rind of your smile.

The fresh pulp gives way to instinct.
Sweet Lilith! I pull you to me,
the sea in your eyes watering, drowning
the flowering flesh under my mouth.

A moment in the garden of your soul,
a walk along the orchard of your body's offering,
a drink from this tributary bursting of life,
and I will believe Eden was once yours.

A Taste of Her

She tastes of heather
from spring,
and pumpkin pie
from fall,
and in her veins pumps
tomorrow for me,
today.
She smells of roses
from summer,
and honeysuckle
from the window,
and in her veins blooms
tomorrow for me,
now.
She sounds like rain,
Autumn storming,
puddling,
warmly flowing,
and in her veins ebbs
yesterday for me,
tonight.
She carries midnight,
in enigmatic smiles,
eyes like comets,
blazing,
and in her veins love
becomes my season,
completely.
She feels like a dove,
downy and silken,
with flesh born for
tenderness,
and in her veins forgiveness
covers my yesterdays -
(and all of my history) -
forever.

An UNstory
(In honor of Bram Stoker)

Universal, understood, underground.
Undulating, unmitigated, unearthly.
Unexpected, unhallowed, unfleshly.
Unholy!

Uncurtained, undraped, unsnarled.
Unbound, uncrated, unsealed.
Undefined, unopened, unsavory.
UNTOMBED!

Unmasked, unveiled, unfettered.
Unaltered, unchanged, undecayed.
Unquestioned, unnoticed, unguarded.
UNLEASHED!

Unprecedented, untimely, unimagined.
Unpopular, unmentioned, undiscovered.
Unrealistic, unspoken, uneventful.
Unjustified!

Unseen, unheard, unwary.
Unnatural, unhappy, unafraid.
Unchristened, unsexed, unyielding.
UNFED!

Unsleeping, untiring, unmourned.
Unshaken, untold, unknown.
Unshadowed, untrue, unending.
UNDEAD!

Unforgotten, unbosomed, unresisted.
Unorthodox, unmoral, untenable.
Unchallenged, unsolved, unbelievable.
Unless…?

The Soul's Sangria

Stilling the mind,
stalling the heart,
embracing the oblivion
under a shroud
of secret regrets.
Cradling the mind,
a pillow for hope,
enduring the forbidden.
Shame wars with rapture
and sanguine fear.
Panic numbs as
diurnal guardians
flower the calyx,
punctuating the remorse
of the seasonless initiate
converted to night,
condemned to sleep
without death, in imitation
of a pentimento life.

Sensory Deprivation

Give me visions; force me into sublime regret.
Lead me into shadowed reveries of a kiss.
Give me whispers; show me the simplicity of sweat.
Grant me your body's loneliness; taste me like this.

Give me ambition; shackle me with quivering lips.
Guide me into whimsical allegory of sinewy combat.
Take my dreams; expose your flippancy in flesh.
Grant me orgiastic illusion; feel me like that.

Goodbye, My Darkness

I weep the silence.
I melody up each full moon, another memory
revisited on ruthless mouths, forgotten kisses of my neuroses.
My eyes scan crowds for an untasted breath,
and orbs, green like fields where I have rested in visions.
A car, the same as yours, or so you said,
rumbles past like some wanton beast. I search
for possibilities, not knowing you, you see.
Your smile, a dreamy softness, a false quilt.
I shiver in the tease of those parted silken lips.
In a stadium of five thousand I'm eager to glimpse
something unrecognizable to anyone but me,
even if I do believe otherwise.

This is for an open window to a forsaken boulevard,
knowing you are out there slamming doors,
bartering the turned away, hoping for the something more
which always will be a little less than what you knew.
This is for the way I recline in pain, beggared in need.
You must return, deny escape into hemorrhagic avenues
where trust is ornamental and requisite to claim a taste of tears.
This is for the crowd, where every smile is given to every face
yet I am the beloved stranger basking in averted eyes -
eyes which lick the silence, shouted over necrotic lips,
lamenting for the hummed anguish we share, inglorious.
I will cross the street now, stumbling away from you,
and close the window to the deaf cacophony, shrill in muteness.
And this, finally, we will call "love."

His Promise

Above a ragged cliff, his raven flies alone.
The moist and sticky winds of ravaged time
lift his despair to abysmal heights.
Emotional currents twist his feathered heart
as acute and pining eyes search for
abandoned hope and forgotten rapture.
Predator he'll always be without a tender hand
to stroke his gentleness disguised in pain.
The gloom will be his only vista
without devotion to call him home.
It is an old and borrowed tale,
where love is dashed on jagged rocks,
and remorseful shards bleed the memories.
Why should the call of night make him quail,
or desolate promises make him fear?
Could be the heavens were meant for lovers,
and his moon is singularly shallow,
unable to illuminate the day?
With determined purpose he turns to midnight,
and wings his bartered dreams on northern gales
where a dove lies in downy charm,
trembling for a pluck of talons.
Rejoice! His oblivion must answer,
because death is all our expectations.
Close your eyes, little dove.
Dream of displaced, honeyed sunsets.
A storm is forming on River Styx,
and in its wake, his raven comes.

Sigh of the Zephyr

Darkly written on an ageless breeze,
Time's essence weeps with evening dew
to tantalize and promise that similarly
the kiss of thorn and rose will come for you.

Arise to an older melody of pulsing heat,
where mortal voices no longer whisper long,
and ghosts are but a legend to the gravestone.
Awaken to the preternatural song!

The illusion is your petals wait for withering.
Nay, my dear, you shrivel only in neglect,
waiting to be pricked with passionate infusion
of blood and song, a naïve prospect.

Close your eyes, surrender to the growing storm.
The zephyr's breath is a sorrowful caress.
It hums a wild dream but ultimately sings alone,
until Night arrives and wraps you in her blessedness.

In Death Repeat

With severed hands, tongue, and mangled heart,
into the denizens presumption fled,
too weak to crawl back; too apathetic to believe.
When does the longing cease to beg?
I've no memory left to bleed, my misanthropic muse.
Forgotten, I simply fade to ebon,
nailed upon passion's rack,
stretched beyond discerning,
where screams are mawkish songs
sung without my listening pride,
surrendered in naked honesty,
rewarded by pity's humiliation,
discarded as a used afterthought of me.
Who craves love's poison sip
when the heart's a sated lover?
Only the thirsty and deranged,
like leftover poltergeists mewling
for yesterday's flamboyant yielding.
Silence is a waking sleep, a better life
though undeserved, devoid of lucid thought,
where bearing painless witness
to imprinted kisses o'er cold flesh
remains blissful torture,
touched upon by ghostly fingers,
unbearable in mutilated ecstasy,
memory quickened, inevitably fractured,
tasteless in a doubting nothingness,
hacked apart in ego's fury -
oh to weep, kneeling in humanity again!
Embrace me in your tomorrow's disdain;
remember me to folly's gluttony
born in the marrow of a wretched night,
incapacitated by this eternal hunger,
eviscerating revenant innocence and desire,
until death relieves me.
Passing unnoticed is enough for sighs
or smiles or immortality in requiem,
when Eternally Yours is a corpse,
an inscription on an empty grave,
or a long forgotten promise in a faithless prayer.

A Scar is Born

First, the lash. A tickle, a tingle and tearing,
curling over flesh in teasing, as if to please or
tantalize. How sweet the moment of anticipation
before the pain.

Then, the wound. A whisper, a wail and a wincing,
searing into flesh, wantonly as if to lease a
wishing. How still the moment of realization
after the pain.

Blood seeks to dance, distracting, devouring
delight in decadence, too distant from the heart
where doubt and desire dwell in the dichotomy of
the silent scream.

Lips will lick the latent lashing, last to lose their
shock, latticed over longing, while levitation of the
limb is promised pain too loud for listening to
lessons of the lost.

Finally, the healing. A harsh and harlot hardening,
forcing two sides to harbor hope against the hush
and hurt, where flesh is both horror and whore to
the homeless heart.

Tomorrow, the memory. A mirror, motive, and milking,
mutilation for the multitudes to muse and muster
motivations. How sweet the mindless misconceptions
excused as misbegotten.

The last lesson is over, the moment begun;
once torn, the damage cannot be undone.
Make no emotional investment in skin.
The only real scars remain within.

For All Time

Who are we, after all,
who seek to bend the intractable,
consoling misery with tears,
eating the stone of our sorrows
until we lick blood from our lips?

You are the soft, yielding desire,
unfolding and ardent,
frightened only by possibilities
and storms without thunder.
Pleasure isn't whole until pain
becomes companionable.
Let this be the last scar I create,
swallowed in our fading bruises.

This is for Then when nights were emergence,
when hollow hearts were insecure
and roses bloomed in the wilds of our fear,
where Night was your sadist and savior,
calling for release and apology,
dancing as mistress and mortician,
when sighs were unnecessary auguries,
and kisses, our anemic ambrosia.

Mine is the irony of failed illusion,
hope betrayed by rotting reality,
lost in the passion, left in the garden,
driven by thirst, moved by reluctance.
I never lied but the truth was destructive,
bowing to denial and consumed like pain,
fortified by a symphony of loneliness,
devoured and tasted with eager delight.

Ours was a union destined for deliverance.
One conclusion and final treachery,
intimately shaped into death's finite blessing.
We are the strong, born out of darkness,
lost in the fold of the failing and weak,
consumed by possession, both of us chained
to the pure and the sanguine,
commanded and guarding eternity's myth.

Withering flower, snapped from the vine,
everything holy turns bitter in blood.
Come to me now, my mortal divinity,
allow us to die in your willing surrender,
my beatitude, my triumph of ultimate selfishness.
One kiss goodbye - oh your eyes, your lips! -
the soul that I coveted, the heart I imagined,
the body I delivered to remorse, at last mine!

Who are we after all, molding our cynicism,
rationalizing our immorality
with a scythe of sweet dreams?
This is the answer, twin spires of destruction.
You are my life, which died in the moment -
shredded of petals, eaten by thorns,
marvelous masochism of hubris and dependency -
that love might continue and live evermore.

In order for the light to shine so brightly,
the darkness must be present.
- Francis Bacon

©Shutterstock 2014

Midnight Assassin, an excerpt

ఞ ఞ

The brass bell over the oak door at the Plates-A-Plenty restaurant announced us and, naturally, almost everyone turned to get a look at the newcomers. Heavy footsteps approached while I pushed the oversized door closed. When I turned around, I couldn't help smiling at the plump and exuberant woman who waved her dishtowel at us.

"As I live and breathe! Temperance Eleonora!" The owner, Miss Margaret, barreled around the corner of the counter, delight sparkling in her eyes. She opened her arms and literally smothered Tempie in one of her famous bear hugs. Her limp dishtowel hung from her fingers, forgotten, as she patted my twin's back. "Saint preserve us, Terry, you brought her after all. Baby Pie, it is so good to see you! It feels like it's been forever." she sighed, her voice fading as she enveloped my sister.

"Oh Momma Maggie!"

I was dumbstruck at how my sister's voice changed, morphing her from the snotty, high-heel debutante into a love-starved, sweet-natured, 10-year-old because of one hug.

Tempie nestled into Margaret's arms. I sidestepped out of the way of others who clamored to say their hello's as one-by-one the customers recognized my sister. Once upon a childhood, our mother had been a close friend to Miss Margaret and Victor, her husband.

Much of the neighborhood remembered us as the little kids who burst in after every Sunday mass. Feet dangling over the edge of black plastic stools, we slurped Italian ices or sundaes while our mother socialized over pie and coffee. It was the only time I remember Mother offering outsiders a genuinely warm smile – ever – and the only time our dad never interfered. Those days were kind; the family allowed us to be children and it was the main reason why we loved Miss Margaret. She was always more of a mother to us than our own had been, especially when it came to love, patience, and lessons.

As the neighborhood feted my sister, I backed out of the boisterous crowd. "I'll grab a booth, T!" I called over heads and turned to claim a table. The store was so crowded at the front that I was forced deeper into the diner, toward the booths.

She was there, leaning against a table, smirking at me, her eyes blazing a lurid green. Tall and imposing, she oozed energy but was motionless, save for that red hair of hers and those damned neon eyes. I frowned, and went to approach her when one of the diners grabbed me by the shoulder and spun me around.

"Teddy, my boy! You're part of this too. Come here, son, and tell us how your dear Mother is doing." Surprise held me fast but I tried to smile and nod at a man I didn't remember while also trying to extricate myself from his grip. I craned my neck to keep eyes on my strange follower. I had to speak with her!

Why does time go so slowly when you're in a hurry? When I finally broke free, she was gone again. I muttered a curse under my breath and pressed past the crowd to the exit, ignoring the door's angry bang and the stupid, clanging bell.

Several people openly objected as I shoved my way through a crowded sidewalk but I ignored their rude comments and scanned every face. Frustration makes you sloppy. Desperation makes you reckless. I knew better but didn't really care. My blood was up.

"Hey! HEY!" I yelled at everyone and no one while searching for the trademark hair that was now so familiar. Dammit. Nothing!

Irritation kept me rooted outside despite my fading hope that I'd see her. I really wanted to throttle my mysterious annoyance. Yup, I really wanted to hit something. When Tempie came out looking for me, her face suggested that I might be overreacting.

"Brother?" Affection gave her voice a new softness. "What is it?" She studied my face. Reluctantly, I faced her. Her hand slid down my arm into my clenched fingers, warm and coaxing. Worry glowed behind her beautiful blue eyes and I had to close mine so she didn't see my fury and let it ruin her moment.

"She was here, T. That *woman.* She was here and she was goading me." I could barely get the words out; so I forced them over my teeth.

"Seriously? Bitch! What did she say? I'll gut her like a fish!" Immediately the kitten became a tiger, her baby blues turning to cold steel. I shook my head, pulling my hand out of her tightening claws.

"Nothing. She's playing with me, that's all. Whoever she is, we have to get this done and then I doubt I'll see her again." *Did I really believe that?* I gave a last look down both sides of the street and waved at Sal (who I noted with some embarrassment was staring at me, eyebrows into his hairline). *Had Sal seen her? I would check with him later.*

Nervous glances continued to pass over us. "We can't do this out here." I said. People were too curious and I felt exposed.

"We'll track her down, Terry. Don't worry. But come in and eat. Maggie's supper's getting cold." Tempie said as I guided her back inside. But I swear I heard laughter in my ear as the door closed behind us.

The rest of dinner went well enough but I couldn't taste it. Tempie gobbled like a real woman, no bird-like eating tonight. The house wine flowed generously and Margaret spoiled us with a mountain of spaghetti topped by her famous veal meatballs. Normally, I'd eat two large helpings but tonight I was full of bitterness and adrenaline. I didn't touch my wine. My stomach was holding drag races and eventually heartburn overtook my appetite.

When we finally left the restaurant, the clock tower bells tolled 9:15. All the way home, my contented sister chatted about the diner folks, who she saw and what she remembered. I let her ramble without interruptions. My mind was on my assignment and my stalker plus I was busy scouting ahead for signs of trouble. As we crossed the street to our block, I was about to comment when suddenly I stopped and pulled Tempie up short.

"Terry? What's...?" I put a finger to her lips as my left arm gathered her against me. Surreptitiously as possible, I guided us into the shadows of a darkened storefront, moving us together as if we were a couple. I prayed to be invisible and ignored. Once concealed, I pointed across and down the road ahead, keeping her mouth covered.

"Needles." I whispered in a breath and Tempie tensed as we cowered together, watching.

"Needles" Puzzoli always arrived with great fanfare. That's why he liked his white caddy. However, tonight he'd upgraded to a white limo. It screamed "pimp," but he believed it shouted "money." It was also why he wore custom Italian suits. Armani was as common for him as a pair of Dockers was for me. Tonight was no exception. I did envy him his suits.

Puzzoli stepped out of his white whale. The light of the "club" reflected off the car's chrome, detailing his shiny patent shoes. *Green* patent. *Who wore crap like that?* But there he was, his shoes matching a green shirt and a darker green tie, stuffed in a bright, white suit. He looked like a stupid cream mint, like the ones in Mom's candy dishes. Needles capped off his look with a white fedora. The hat mirrored one our father used to wear but his was a too small for his big head and he wore it cocked back. I smothered a laugh and then nearly choked. The main event followed him out of the car.

Serious arm candy emerged from the limo wearing a slick green dress made to cling to all the sexiest parts of a woman's body. And, man, what a body! I saw stilettos with those famous red soles. They're the ones Tempie goes stupid over. Then, legs that seemed to travel all the way to her neck poured out from a thigh high slit in her dress. Pale, long arms, delicate hands without painted nails. Classy. And, whoa, the woman was taller than Needles in her heels, standing well over six foot two or three! T and I both gaped in appreciation.

The last thing I noticed was the mass of serious red hair that seemed to float with a life of its own...

Oh hell, you have to be *kidding* me! The woman attempting to edge me out of my kill was standing, devil-may-care, smack next to Needles, smiling down at him as if he were her private, minty-fresh dessert. My vision turned red.

Needles never noticed Tempie and me; he was too preoccupied with his eye candy. But *she* saw me. A slight tilt of her head, a sideways glance, and I swear those unmistakable eyes narrowed in warning.

Suddenly, my first decision moment arrived out of accidental necessity. When Temperance saw Needles, my sweet-natured sister became a deadly killer with vengeance to serve and justice to mete out.

Tempie smoothly shoved me aside as she honed in on Needles and his "companion." With practiced nonchalance, she stepped off the sidewalk and into the shadows between streetlights. Her intention was obvious; she would use the blind spots to approach Needles. Who would pay attention to a lovely woman in ordinary clothes going for a stroll? Her facial expression was as deliberately indifferent as her walk.

I panicked. It wasn't fear, you understand, or anything sexist. I figured Tempie was as good an assassin as any I knew but she used a knife. That meant she had to get close enough to Needles to...

I never finished the thought.

It was like a lightning strike. Before Tempie got within fifty feet of the car, Needles was inside, the entourage was gone, and Tempie found herself knocked to the ground. In a blink, we were alone.

I ran to my sister when she cried out in surprise.

"She...she cut me! That bitch *cut* me!" She brought her hand away from her face, and as I knelt beside her, I noticed a thin slice at the bottom of her chin. My heart stopped.

Anxiously I glanced around then brushed her hair aside, turning her head toward the streetlight. "Dammit, let me see!" I studied her. "Small. I don't think there will be a scar but what in the hell did you think you were doing?" I wanted to shake her. Instead I took a deep breath and helped her to her feet. But I hadn't finished venting. "That was really stupid, Temps! You could have ruined all my hard work!" She gave me a withering look. "Yeah, okay and gotten killed " She nodded at that, mollified. "But how do you know the woman cut you?" It was too wild to imagine.

At the last, Temperance's face paled. Slowly, she wiped away more blood with shaky hands that grabbed at me.

"Terry, I'm telling you it was your woman. She cut me and she said something to me, too."

Her eyes showed more white than color as she stared at me. Shock was setting in. I couldn't figure any other reason for her wild accusation. Still, something was too strange and uncomfortable about the whole incident. *Why would she want to hurt my sister?*

"Ok, T, I'll bite. What did this very fast, very dangerous woman, not mine by the way - who somehow managed to become friends with Needles, who, by the way, hasn't a clue who you are, somehow managed to cut you and speak to you without either of us actually seeing it - say to you?"

Tempie closed her eyes, leaned her head against my chest, and whispered, "Next time, you die."

❧ ❧

One thing I've learned from our family, killing is a cold business. To succeed at what I do, you must out-think the other person. You must possess a second more of patience, a moment less of anger, and be more ruthless and cunning than your opponent. To be a killer means laying aside your basic instincts and serving one mistress: Death.

Back at my place, I mulled over our mess of a situation as I put antiseptic on my sister's chin. She tried to be a trooper but the incident clearly shook her confidence. Temps was vain enough to worry about a scar, though she pretended not to care. But another part of her was angry. Unfortunately, not angry enough to keep her safe. Not nearly enough. She left that to me, so I considered my options.

Whoever this woman was, she was well-trained. She was always ahead of me. She had ingratiated herself into Needles' world and excluded us. She forced us to stand aside when it was obvious she knew what we - what I - was about and she didn't care. Now, she threatened us. Out of all this, I had to swallow my fury, and lock down my timetable. Somehow, I had to work around this woman or I'd have to kill her, too.

After Tempie drank some of her god-awful herbal tea, she fell asleep. Around one in the morning, I was watching out the window again when the limo returned. Needles' ridiculous entourage emerged from his dive and dispersed into their darkened cars. Finally, after the crowd died away, *she* stepped out with Needles, clinging to his side. I grabbed my binoculars and studied her. Even in the dull street light, she radiated an aura of something strangely otherworldly She was too beautiful, like a forgery that is too perfect. You notice it but you don't know why.

They lingered over a kiss as she stroked Needles' face before she tucked him into his car. I wanted to gag. Curiously, Needles seemed dazed and dulled. I can't be sure, but I thought he whimpered as she closed his door and she laughed. The sound carried like tiny bells lifted on a breeze from far away. A hauntingly memorable echo that gave me goose flesh.

The limo and all the other cars drove off and left her standing alone on the empty sidewalk. The street was completely deserted. When the last car disappeared, an odd quiet descended. She stepped into the street, her stilettos sounding sharp in the cool air. When she reached midway, she looked up, directly at my window, and spoke - *spoke* - to me, in a voice like a thousand angry whispers. This ugly sound, however, pulsed only in my head, which I gripped in surprise.

Come down or I come up.

As suddenly as it came, the voice (and my pain) was gone and she disappeared from view. I turned to wake Temps when another wave hit my head and nearly knocked me on my knees.

Alone. The word slammed into me like a truck.

Commanded, confused and pissed as being bossed, I tucked my Ruger in my jeans' waist. Insurance. With a glance at my sleeping sister, I slid down the fire escape, landing in the side street. There were no streetlights here. Caution didn't make me stupid even if it brought momentary restraint!

I never believed in Halloween or ghost stories. I stopped going to church because I didn't believe in the idea of demons or the boogeyman either. However, what I saw next brought all my convictions up short.

This "woman" drifted out of the shadows, shadows that looked alive as they writhed and twisted about her body like something in a slow motion video. That amazing red hair lifted and coiled around her face as if the wind constantly buffeted her. *Damn, she was hot!* Without meaning to, I gasped and I fell into her eyes. Those eyes I'd seen up close promised depths of the hottest summers yet crackled with veins of ice. *What are you?*

We had to be over a hundred feet apart but the menace radiated off her as she moved toward me. She made no sound. In fact, the night seemed inexplicably dead.

Dead. *Shit!* I reached behind me and gripped my gun. Instinctively, I backed up.

In a blink, she closed the distance between us. Cold washed over me and I tasted rust on the air, before I smelled something sickly sweet.

"What are you?" I croaked, choking on my own senses.

"You know what I am, honey. You've feared what you thought you knew since the first time you saw me. Don't play with me; I might like it too much." She tilted her head as she stared at me, smirking and unblinking. Her flesh was nearly transparent and as much I wanted to touch her, anger won.

"*Know you*? I don't know you, bitch. You've played with me, threatened me, and got in my way and now you attack my sister? I don't know who you are or what you want but …" I started to pull the gun.

She laughed again, a sound so odd and beautiful but it stabbed me like a hard freeze. The sardonic amusement compounded when she lowered her head and whispered, "Come here, honey."

My body went rigid. The gun slipped from my fingers and I watched as it fell away. With feet of lead, I walked toward her unwillingly and I couldn't stop a sigh of pleasure when she wrapped me in her arms.

"Who are you? What are you?" I nearly moaned as her body touched mine and her face drew closer. Her wet, red lips invited and made it hard to concentrate or remember where I was.

"You know what I am. I am you. We are the same, Terry. I am a killer, just like you."

I shook my head, trying to shake off this lethargy I felt near her. I knew what she said was wrong but my head couldn't find any words to argue with her. Her fingers slipped into my hair and pulled my head back.

"No, not…the…same." I panted every word as her lips traced behind my ear, down my face to my jaw. I shuddered.

"Ssh, yes, we are. I am you. I am not like your sister. Your sister isn't you. You and me, we're alike, honey. By the Benj, don't you see? We are assassins. We are closer than brother and sister because we share a need for blood. We want the same thing; we crave it. We should work together…" Her mouth worked against my cheek and every word punctured my heart.

A trained killer studies possible outcomes: what to do if captured, how to play against your attacker, or what to do if ambushed. This was an ambush and I struggled to make sense of her words, to shake the compulsion that held me in a vice. She wanted to talk, so I talked, moving my head from side to side.

"Work…work with you? Are you nuts?" My mouth worked the words and it felt like chewing fuzz. "What did you do to me, bitch? Drugs? That's what Needles paid you to do, isn't it? Are you his whore now?"

She released me and my head jerked. Then, *pain.* She slapped me. My jaw connected with her hand, the rock. Didn't see that coming.

Just like that, the world tilted on its axis. The warmth and lust I imagined disappeared into a stinging fog of airless crimson. Eyes that had beckoned suddenly sparkled with green frost. Arms that were pliant and caressing turned into marble vices. The lilting voice became deep and harsh. I felt, more than I knew, that I was, quite literally, about to die.

For one moment, red shadows smothered me and I couldn't see anything but two neon green orbs hovering over me. I gasped for air that wasn't there.

"Little man, what a predictable disappointment you are. I liked you so I dealt openly with you and your childish game of 'killer pawns.' I warned you and you ignored me. Now you will hear me. The man is *mine.* I don't care what you want or why. Don't make me have to kill you or your sister. It would be too easy; I prefer a challenge. I'm most dangerous when bored."

For one second, I glimpsed something in her face that I still don't believe I saw. The next, she tossed me like an empty beer bottle. I flew across the street, landing unceremoniously on a trash bag at the curb. As I righted myself, she charged me. Scrambling fast, I reached for my gun and then realized it was still lying in the street!

She bore down on me, seeming to float over the wet street, hair flying, eyes burning, and mouth open. If there really were demons, in that moment I believed in the beauty of evil, of dark things that men should never know. She hovered over me and, from what I witnessed in her face, well, I nearly pissed myself. For once, I knew exactly what it was to face down Death. I was terrified speechless and I cowered from what I thought I saw.

And that's when she lowered herself down on my body and licked my face again. Seriously.

I went stiff with shock and disgust. I rubbed my cheek, and tried to ignore the onslaught of desire that screamed NOTICE ME. Her amused voice drifted like a breeze buffeting the walls of the building and lingered over me. I put a hand over my groin, strictly protectively, of course. She laughed!

"Mmm, maybe next time, honey. If you heed my warning."

Then, like before, she simply disappeared. A blink and nothing remained but shifting shadows. I sat there for a moment, playing emotional spin the bottle and brushed my face again in disbelief. I felt branded and exposed. My brain hated her and my body screamed for want of her.

I don't know how long it was before I could get myself off the trash heap and back inside. Time didn't resonate or seem relevant anymore. I struggled to make sense of it all including the threat to our lives. How would I explain to Tempie what I didn't understand or believe myself?

Who in the blue blazes of the seven hells was she? I kept asking but there were never any answers. Again, I touched my face, remembering her mouth against my skin and how she looked, so hideously enraged.

Suddenly light bulbs popped everywhere.

I knew. I mean *I knew* even if I didn't dare say it aloud. She was damned scary and yet so beautiful it was hard to grasp. There was a faint hint of something foul, but I thought I imagined it. Her breath was so sweet, the mouth that I wanted to both kiss and slap, so ripe with a hint of *something*. I'm certain I saw, like an animal - no! Not possible.

I scanned up and down the street as the clock chimed 4:45. I warred with my thoughts but gradually my disbelief crumbled into impossible reality. I thought of her laughing and suddenly I wanted to laugh, too.

Still shaking, I returned to my building, took the stairs four at a time (felt like it) and stopped dead (heh) beside my sister's snoring form. I tried very hard to hold it together. I wanted to scream and shake her. I wanted to hurt something but holy hells, how did I deal with this?

"T! Temperance." I tried my outside voice. "TEMPIE. Wake. Up!"

Normally my sister can sleep through an explosion. Something in the sharpness of my voice, perhaps mixed with my absolute calm, roused her. Her hand reached under her pillow (instinct drew her to her knife) and her eyes focused on me. Nothing else about her moved; she barely breathed.

"What is it, Terry?" Her voice was thick with sleep, wary.

"I've seen her again. *The woman.* I met her." I giggled.

At this point my legs wobbled so badly that I simply collapsed on the floor. My twin watched me go down, then sat up violently awake.

"I asked you before, what is it about this bitch, Terry? I can rip her eyes out, just say the word."

"No sister, you can't. I can't. Needles can't. Even Sal can't. I doubt anyone can." Hysteria kicked in; I started giggling and couldn't stop.

Temperance tumbled out of bed and knelt in front of me. She shook me so hard my teeth rattled. I glanced at her though a watery fog.

"Dammit, what's wrong with you? I thought you said she was just another assassin looking to make a kill." Tempie was so serious! I laughed even harder, whooping like a lunatic and starting to hiccup. It was a relief to let go.

She drew back and gaped at me while I gripped my sides and hooted. I felt badly for her confusion but I knew I couldn't help her.

"Noooo..." I hiccupped harder and waved her off. "But she is going to kill, I'm sure of that."

"Why? And what's so funny? Does she want Needles, is that it?"

Tempie's question sent me into more sidesplitting, uncontrollable belly laughs of terror and the tears raced down my cheeks. I felt marked, so I didn't try to wipe them. Maybe they'd wash my face clean again. Otherwise, nothing much mattered. *Maybe Sal could help.*

My twin frowned at me, frustrated. *Here goes nothing.*

"Vampire." I whispered with yet another hiccup.

A stunned twin blinked at me as if I'd just threatened her with some bargain brand shoe. Meanwhile, my imagination danced with shadows.

Tonight at 6. They found him in the street, two puncture wounds in his neck, his body drained of blood. What killed him, Inspector Clouseau?

"A vampire," I repeated and glanced around the room. I half expected - well, you know - and laughed harder as Tempie screamed.

©Shutterstock 2014

About the Author

Sherry Rentschler's poetry has appeared online and in print. Her work includes assistant poetry editor for an online poetry magazine, newspaper columnist and photojournalist. A bit of an adventurer, Rentschler lived in Italy for a few years, which allowed her to travel around Europe and the Middle East. Her other travels include visits to the Caribbean, Puerto Rico, and Greenland.

Among her hobbies are all things vampire, plus dragon collecting, photographing trees, and dancing with faeries. An avid fan of old Sherlock Holmes movies, she also enjoys reading urban and gothic fantasies, savoring fine wines, and rich, dark chocolates. Rentschler is a retired USAF veteran and currently resides in North Carolina with her husband, also a retired USAF veteran.

This is Rentschler's second poetry collection. Her first, *Paper Bones*, is a 2014 National Indie Excellence Award (NIEA) Finalist, a 2014 Global Ebook Award Gold Medalist, a 2014 Readers' Favorite International Book Award Finalist, and a 2013 Best Cover Award Gold Medalist from AUTHORSdB.

Facebook.com/AuthorSherryRentschler
Follow @poetphoenix on Twitter
Share books lists on Goodreads.com/poetphoenix

CPSIA information can be obtained at www.ICGtesting.com
Printed in the USA
BVOW11*2034061014

369752BV00001B/1/P